DINNER TABLE DEVOTIONS

DINNER Table DEVOTIONS

40 DAYS
OF SPIRITUAL NOURISHMENT
FOR YOUR FAMILY

NANCY GUTHRIE

TYNDALE
MOMENTUM®

The Tyndale nonfiction imprint

Visit Tyndale online at tyndale.com.

Visit Tyndale Momentum online at tyndalemomentum.com.

Visit Nancy Guthrie's website at nancyguthrie.com.

TYNDALE, Tyndale's quill logo, *Tyndale Momentum*, the Tyndale Momentum logo, and *The One Year* are registered trademarks of Tyndale House Ministries. *One Year* and The One Year logo are trademarks of Tyndale House Ministries. Tyndale Momentum is the nonfiction imprint of Tyndale House Publishers, Carol Stream, Illinois.

Dinner Table Devotions: 40 Days of Spiritual Nourishment for Your Family

Copyright © 2021 by Nancy Guthrie. All rights reserved.

Adapted from *One Year of Dinner Table Devotions and Discussion Starters* published in 2008 under ISBN 978-1-4143-1895-0.

Cover photograph of plate on checkered tablecloth copyright © Jiri Hera/Shutterstock. All rights reserved.

Author photograph copyright © 2018 by Eric Brown. All rights reserved.

Designed by Gearbox

Edited by Stephanie Rische

Unless otherwise indicated, all Scripture quotations are taken from the *Holy Bible*, New Living Translation, second edition, copyright © 1996, 2004, 2007 by Tyndale House Foundation. (Some quotations may be from the NLT, first edition, copyright © 1996.) Used by permission of Tyndale House Publishers, Carol Stream, Illinois 60188. All rights reserved.

Scripture quotations marked NIV are taken from the Holy Bible, *New International Version*,® *NIV*.® Copyright © 1973, 1978, 1984 by Biblica, Inc.® Used by permission. All rights reserved worldwide.

Scripture quotations marked NASB are taken from the New American Standard Bible,® copyright © 1960, 1962, 1963, 1968, 1971, 1972, 1973, 1975, 1977, 1995 by The Lockman Foundation. Used by permission.

Scripture verses marked *Phillips* are taken from *The New Testament in Modern English* by J. B. Phillips, copyright © J. B. Phillips, 1958, 1959, 1960, 1972. All rights reserved.

For information about special discounts for bulk purchases, please contact Tyndale House Publishers at csresponse@tyndale.com, or call 1-855-277-9400.

ISBN 978-1-4964-5087-6

Printed in the United States of America

27 26 25 24 23 22 21
7   6   5   4   3   2   1

INTRODUCTION

Most modern Christian families live with a nagging sense of guilt that they don't have any kind of consistent family devotions. Or maybe I should say *my husband and I* have lived with a nagging sense of guilt that we have not had any kind of consistent family devotions! But I don't think we're alone in this.

Getting the kids to turn off the TV and computer and gather to read the Bible, to have a meaningful discussion everybody participates in, and to pray over anything other than a meal seems like too much of a daily hurdle for most families. Besides, most of us don't feel like we are authorities on the Bible, so we hardly know where to start. But we want to do something. And we want more than a daily chore that our children dread and can't wait to be done with. We're looking for something that won't be resisted or rejected as "totally lame." We want a meaningful and personal discussion about things that really matter, something everyone takes part in.

That's why I originally wrote *One Year of Dinner Table*

Devotions and Discussion Starters, and that is why we've adapted it into this convenient forty-day version. *Dinner Table Devotions* helps families start in a natural gathering place—around the dinner table. As the meal comes to a close, family members can take turns reading the dinner table devotion. Each devotion includes readings on a specific theme from two or three Scripture passages out of the accessible New Living Translation, a brief devotional thought, and three discussion-starter questions—all designed to be done together as a family in ten to fifteen minutes (before everybody helps with the kitchen cleanup!). You'll also find space to make notes. Your family can use this space in a number of ways, including to record your kids' comments and questions, matters for prayer for each other, things you want to thank and praise God for, and new discoveries you've made about Christ and the Christian life.

It is written for families with children in all stages—from elementary school to high school—who long for a way to have spiritual input in their children's lives and who want Scripture to be naturally woven into their family life and conversations.

WHAT MAKES *DINNER TABLE DEVOTIONS* DIFFERENT?

Whereas most family devotionals focus on Bible stories or on practical moral lessons, *Dinner Table Devotions* focuses on biblical themes, concepts, and words—in ways that are understandable to children without talking down to adults or teens. It will help your family take a step back to look at the big picture of what God is doing in the world and his purposes and plans in creating and redeeming the world. Once you and your family have worked your way through this book, you will have discussed many different attributes of God and explored what it really means to be joined to Jesus Christ by faith. This is not dry theology for theology's sake, but living theology that makes a huge difference in how we do battle against temptation, deal with disappointment, and determine our futures.

Over the course of the next forty days, your family will go deeper into developing an understanding of who God is, what he is like, what he expects, and what he is doing. Together you can embark on a journey of understanding who we are, why we need a Savior, and what it means to place our faith solely in Jesus. Holy living flows out of that.

The format of a short devotion followed by three discussion questions is designed to turn the devotional time into a family-wide discussion rather than a one-person lecture or reading. This is not a continuation of the school day or Sunday school but an opportunity to apply biblical truths to the most important areas of life.

HOW TO USE *DINNER TABLE DEVOTIONS*

If you've rarely read and discussed God's Word together as a family, it can be awkward at first. But that initial awkwardness fades as conversations are sparked and understanding deepens. We have a treasure to pass on to our children—the Bible, which contains God's message to us and the answers to life's greatest questions. Because it is so important to us, we want to talk about it.

The goal of these devotions is to create an opportunity for dialogue and conversation. You as a parent set the tone as you allow yourself to be a learner and a seeker rather than a teacher or an authority. You do this as you are willing to say, "I don't think I really understand that completely" or "That is something I'd like to work on in my life to be more like Jesus." You do this as you affirm the input of every family member and maintain an atmosphere of acceptance and open participation.

Perhaps the most important way to encourage your dinner table devotions and discussions is something that happens away from the table. You want to make sure any confession of struggle or weakness expressed in your discussions is treated with respect and confidentiality. Nothing puts the lid on authentic sharing more quickly than when people's words are used against them. The best way to encourage vulnerability and openness is by creating a safe environment for sharing.

Each devotion is designed for everyone around the table to share and interact with it. You might choose to have different family members read the various verses, and you can encourage conversations by discussing the questions at the end of each devotion. The first question is answerable for family members of all ages, elementary and up. It is designed to draw family members in and to get everyone talking about their own thoughts and experiences. The next two questions are more thought provoking and in some cases more personal.

You may want to have different family members read the questions each time so that everyone has an opportunity to be on the asking end and the answering end. Many of the questions are "What do you think?" questions that may or may not have a "right" answer. Some are "Why do you think?" questions meant to encourage deeper thinking. And many are "How?" or "In what ways?" questions meant to draw out practical application of the truths presented. There are no answers in the back of the book! When you come to a question that is challenging to everyone around the table, this presents the opportunity to acknowledge that God is a mystery to be probed and a treasure to be mined, and that the things of God are not always simple to figure out. But the rewards for pursuing them are great.

The most personal questions are those that ask participants to identify ways they need to change or ways they would like to change. This can be new territory for families, but it also presents a meaningful opportunity for family members to connect with each other and with God. As a parent, you can set the tone and example here in terms of a willingness to be humble and to show others in the family that you are still an "unfinished project" when it comes to becoming all God wants you to be.

STARTING THE CONVERSATION

In Deuteronomy 6:6-7, we read this instruction from God to the people of Israel: "You must commit yourselves whole-heartedly to these commands that I am giving you today. Repeat them again and again to your children. Talk about them when you are at home and when you are on the road, when you are going to bed and when you are getting up." What better place to practice "when you are at home" than around the dinner table?

The people of Israel were expected to understand Scripture well enough to talk about it with their children. They were to discuss the words of Scripture during their family activities and apply them to everyday life situations.

Our desire for our kids is that they develop a faith that is real and personal—not something they grow out of or leave behind. When they are pressed by the world, we want them to have the foundation to piece together what their faith really means and what makes Jesus worth knowing and following. We want them to be able to make an argument for him and feel comfortable talking about him as someone who is real, someone who matters in every area of their lives.

Now is the time to begin that conversation so it becomes as natural as breathing. It's by talking about him that we weave our understanding of God through all of life and through the life of our families. As we talk about him, he enters into not only our discussions around the dinner table but also our entertainment choices, our spending habits, our vacations, our time, and certainly our treatment of each other. By bringing him into our discussions around the dinner table, we saturate our lives with God. And isn't that what we really want?

Paul wrote, "Whether you eat or drink, or whatever you do, do it all for the glory of God" (1 Corinthians 10:31). I'm praying for you as you seek to glorify God around your dinner table—that he will be pleased, and that your family will have some laughs, perhaps shed some tears, and grow together toward God.

Nancy Guthrie
Nashville, Tennessee

KNOWING GOD VERSUS KNOWING ABOUT GOD

Those who wish to boast should boast in this alone: that they truly know me and understand that I am the LORD who demonstrates unfailing love and who brings justice and righteousness to the earth, and that I delight in these things. I, the LORD, have spoken!

JEREMIAH 9:24

This is the way to have eternal life—to know you, the only true God, and Jesus Christ, the one you sent to earth.

JOHN 17:3

Everything else is worthless when compared with the infinite value of knowing Christ Jesus my Lord.

PHILIPPIANS 3:8

Do you know your mail carrier? How about your grand-parents? How about the President of the United States? How about your best friend? There are different ways of "knowing" people, aren't there? There are some people we know *about*, but we don't really know them personally. And even among those we know personally, there are different levels of knowing—we know some more intimately than others.

The Bible says that we are made to know God. But a person can know a lot *about* God and not really *know* him. We can be interested in theology (which is a fascinating subject!) and know the books and stories of the Bible, and hardly know God at all. We can go to church and read lots of Christian books and be up on the latest teaching and yet not know God at all.

We get to know other people through personal interaction and involvement, by sharing life with them. We listen to what they say, observe how they interact with others, see what they value, find out what they enjoy. And it is similar with God. As we read and think about and talk about God as he is revealed in the Bible, we get to know him. God is so magnificent that it is worth spending the rest of our lives getting to know him better. As we do so, things that confused us before about what he does and how he works begin to make more sense to us. Knowing him better helps us trust him more.

DISCUSSION STARTERS

- Who are some of the people you know best? How did you get to know them?
- What is the difference between knowing about God and knowing him?
- In what way would you like to know God better than you do right now?

THAT'S NOT FAIR!

When God our Savior revealed his kindness and love, he saved us, not because of the righteous things we had done, but because of his mercy.

TITUS 3:4-5

Have mercy on me, O God, because of your unfailing love. Because of your great compassion, blot out the stain of my sins.

PSALM 51:1

God had mercy on me so that Christ Jesus could use me as a prime example of his great patience with even the worst sinners. Then others will realize that they, too, can believe in him and receive eternal life.

1 TIMOTHY 1:16

We live in a world that teaches us, "The early bird gets the worm," "No pain, no gain," "There is no such thing as a free lunch," and "You get what you pay for." We buy the idea that people get what they deserve, at least in theory. Whenever we experience hardship or difficulty, we quickly say, "I don't deserve this!" Believing we have a right to fairness, we feel violated when we think we haven't gotten what we deserve.

On the surface, a perfectly fair world appeals to us. But would we really want to live in such a world? In a completely fair world, there is no room for grace—receiving what you don't deserve. There would be no room for mercy either—being spared from getting the punishment you do deserve. We deserve punishment but receive forgiveness; we deserve judgment but experience love; we deserve death but get showered with God's mercy.

Since we live in a world where we don't always get what we deserve and where we sometimes get what we don't deserve, we will experience loss. But this also means we can receive mercy. Ultimately it is not "fairness" we want from God. If he gave us what is fair—what we really deserve—we would have to pay for our sins. What we really want from God is justice (doing what is right) and mercy (not giving us the punishment we've earned). And we can be confident that his abundant mercy will keep us from getting what we really deserve.

DISCUSSION STARTERS

- Can you think of a time when you said, "That's not fair"? How do we know what is fair?
- Are there ways God is not fair but is right?
- Do you want other people to treat you with fairness or with grace and mercy? Why?

WE'RE ALL POOR

No one is righteous—not even one. No one is truly wise; no one is seeking God. All have turned away; all have become useless. No one does good, not a single one.

ROMANS 3:10-12

God saved you by his grace when you believed. And you can't take credit for this; it is a gift from God. Salvation is not a reward for the good things we have done, so none of us can boast about it.

EPHESIANS 2:8-9

You say, "I am rich. I have everything I want. I don't need a thing!" And you don't realize that you are wretched and miserable and poor and blind and naked.

REVELATION 3:17

Is there something you really want? Something that you want so much that you are willing to work for it and save for it so you can buy it?

What if what you really want is to be in good standing with God? Can you save up enough good works, enough proper behavior, enough denying yourself to buy God's favor? Unfortunately not. God doesn't accept people who think they have some sort of spiritual currency or money to be able to buy his blessing. In fact, he says that the only people he accepts are those who recognize that they not only don't have enough to offer God, they have absolutely nothing to offer God. "God blesses those who are poor and realize their need for him," Jesus said (Matthew 5:3). He wasn't talking about people who are financially poor but people who are spiritually poor, people who are spiritually bankrupt.

Only when we see that we have nothing to offer God to gain his favor—no family connections, no self-sacrifice, not even any natural tendency to love him—only then are we in a position to receive what God wants to give to us. And then he gives us everything. Jesus is the one who receives all things from God the Father, and he shares all those good things with us. When we come to him with nothing to offer him except for our need, he welcomes us into his family and into the kind of blessing that only he can provide.

DISCUSSION STARTERS

- What would be the most difficult part of being financially poor?
- What does it mean to be poor in spirit? What is the opposite of being poor in spirit?
- Why is it so difficult to admit that we're spiritually poor?

GOD'S TATTOO

Jerusalem says, "The LORD has deserted us; the Lord has forgotten us."

"Never! Can a mother forget her nursing child? Can she feel no love for the child she has borne? But even if that were possible, I would not forget you! See, I have written your name on the palms of my hands. Always in my mind is a picture of Jerusalem's walls in ruins."

ISAIAH 49:14-16

They will see his face, and his name will be written on their foreheads.

REVELATION 22:4

Have you ever seen someone with a person's name tattooed onto an arm or ankle? Some people tattoo the name of the person they love on their bodies as an expression of their devotion to the person, and as a constant reminder of this person who is precious to them.

When God's people complained to God that they thought he had abandoned them, God told them, "I have written your name on the palms of my hands." It's as if he held out his open hands to those who felt forgotten by him and said, "Look. You will see something—someone—too precious to me to ever forget."

If you could look at God's hands, you would see that he has tattooed your name there because he loves you. He wants to keep you in the center of his attention. He thinks about you all the time. He watches over you. When he sees your name there, your concerns become his concerns. He sees not only your name but every aspect of your life—every joy, every struggle, every need. You are never off his mind, out of his sight, or away from his loving care.

DISCUSSION STARTERS

- Do you think you would ever get a tattoo? Why or why not? Does your family have opinions or rules regarding tattoos?
- Have you ever felt like God forgot about you? What are some things you know about God that can give you confidence that he will never abandon you?

- Revelation 22:4 describes people in heaven having Jesus' name on their foreheads. What do you think this imagery of having Jesus' name tattooed on our foreheads is intended to communicate?

_____

_____

_____

_____

_____

_____

_____

_____

_____

_____

ALL EARS

You want what you don't have, so you scheme and kill to get it. You are jealous of what others have, but you can't get it, so you fight and wage war to take it away from them. Yet you don't have what you want because you don't ask God for it.

JAMES 4:2

When you call, the LORD will answer. "Yes, I am here," he will quickly reply.

ISAIAH 58:9

In my distress I prayed to the LORD, and the LORD answered me and set me free.

PSALM 118:5

Have you ever tried to talk to someone who was distracted? Maybe the person was listening to music or reading something or deep in thought, and you felt like he or she was ignoring you.

What about God? Does he ever ignore us when we talk to him? When we pray, can we be confident God will listen and respond in some way, or does he sometimes ignore our prayers? We often wonder if prayer can really change anything. But the Bible promises us that God always listens and that our prayers have an impact on what we receive from God.

When James said, "You don't have what you want because you don't ask God for it," he was implying that our failure to pray and ask God for what we need deprives us of what God would have given us if we'd asked. And when Jesus instructed us to "keep on asking, and you will receive what you ask for" (Matthew 7:7), he was making a clear connection between asking God for things and receiving them from him. So evidently, when we ask God to work in our lives, he responds. That doesn't mean he's like a genie and will automatically give us whatever we want. But he does promise to hear us and respond—even if his response is not the response we were looking for. Even more, as we pray to him, telling him what we need and asking for him to work, sometimes he works to change what we want or to accept what he has given and what he is doing.

God is happy when we depend on him and talk to him. So he never ignores our heartfelt requests for his presence and his power in our lives. In prayer, we take a step in his direction, and he comes close to us. We can be confident that even though other people may ignore us, God never will.

DISCUSSION STARTERS

- Have you ever tried to talk to someone only to have him or her ignore you? How did that feel?
- Have you ever felt like God was ignoring you? When you feel that way, is that really true?
- How have you experienced God's response to your prayers?

DAY 6

DAY 6

ARE YOU CHANGING?

All of us who have had that veil removed can see and reflect the glory of the Lord. And the Lord—who is the Spirit—makes us more and more like him as we are changed into his glorious image.

2 CORINTHIANS 3:18

The LORD your God will change your heart and the hearts of all your descendants, so that you will love him with all your heart and soul and so you may live!

DEUTERONOMY 30:6

This same Good News that came to you is going out all over the world. It is bearing fruit everywhere by changing lives, just as it changed your lives from the day you first heard and understood the truth about God's wonderful grace.

COLOSSIANS 1:6

People can change a lot of things about themselves. They can change their hair color, their names, and the people they spend time with. And there are some things they can't change—certain physical characteristics, the families they came from, and their natural personality types. When it comes to changing our habits or ways of thinking or the ways we respond to things, sometimes we feel powerless. *That's just the way I am*, we think. *I'll never change.*

But we are not on our own when it comes to change. If we are joined to Christ by faith, we can be sure that the Holy Spirit is at work, using the word of God to change us from the inside out. The Holy Spirit is giving us the power we need to say "no" to sins we used to only say "yes" to. Over time, as we keep on turning away from sin and toward Jesus, we discover that we are no longer stuck committing the same old sins and thinking the same destructive thoughts and feeling the same defeated feelings. As we grow in love for Jesus, we find that we love what he loves and hate what he hates. We find that we want to be more like him in every way. It doesn't happen in an instant, but rather over a lifetime. We change. We change to become more like Jesus.

DISCUSSION STARTERS

- How have you changed over the past year? How would you like to change in the coming year?
- What things about yourself do you need to accept as part of the way God made you?
- What things about yourself have you accepted as "just the way you are" that need to be changed to be more like Jesus?

A HIGHER AUTHORITY

The king's heart is like a stream of water directed by
the LORD; he guides it wherever he pleases.

PROVERBS 21:1

Everyone must submit to governing authorities. For
all authority comes from God, and those in positions
of authority have been placed there by God.

ROMANS 13:1

Jesus Christ . . . is the faithful witness to these things,
the first to rise from the dead, and the ruler of all the
kings of the world.

REVELATION 1:5

Open up the newspaper, turn on the television, or look online and you'll read or hear strong opinions about the policies of our government or the people leading our government. And if you listen, you'll probably hear some strong opinions expressed by people at your house about the current president or party in power too.

We sometimes wonder why God would allow a particular person or party to be in power over us—especially when it seems that their agenda is opposed to what we know honors God. But the Bible tells us that, "[God] controls the course of world events; he removes kings and sets up other kings" (Daniel 2:21). All kings (and presidents) are under God's ultimate control. He allows them to be put into office, and he allows them to be taken out of office.

The Bible also tells us to submit to all rulers—including leaders we disagree with, unfair bosses, and corrupt governments. "For the Lord's sake, respect all human authority—whether the king as head of state, or the officials he has appointed" (1 Peter 2:13-14). When we submit to earthly authority, we're submitting for the Lord's sake, to demonstrate our glad obedience to him in all things.

A third thing the Bible teaches us is that God has the power to guide the "king's heart" or to change any leader's mind or policy. This is why we pray for our leaders, even when we don't like what they do, asking God to work in and through them to accomplish whatever he intends.

DISCUSSION STARTERS

- Who is in authority over you? What does it mean to submit to authority?
- How does submitting to the authority of the government show our faith in God?
- Can we disagree with someone in authority and still submit? How?

DOES GOD GET JEALOUS?

You must worship no other gods, for the Lord, whose very name is Jealous, is a God who is jealous about his relationship with you.

EXODUS 34:14

I am jealous for you with the jealousy of God himself. I promised you as a pure bride to one husband— Christ. But I fear that somehow your pure and undivided devotion to Christ will be corrupted.

2 CORINTHIANS 11:2-3

You adulterers! Don't you realize that friendship with the world makes you an enemy of God? . . . If you want to be a friend of the world, you make yourself an enemy of God. What do you think the Scriptures mean when they say that the spirit God has placed within us is filled with envy?

JAMES 4:4-5

Some people call it the "green-eyed monster." It ruins relationships and makes people miserable. What is it? Jealousy. To be jealous is to want what someone else has only for yourself. Paul lists jealousy with other "desires of your sinful nature" (Galatians 5:19-21).

But we also read in the Bible that God is jealous, and it makes us wonder, *If jealousy is bad, how could God describe himself as jealous?*

God's jealousy is not like our self-serving jealousy. He is not out of sorts or irritable because of envy; he is passionate for our affection out of love. God is perfect, and his jealousy for the exclusive affections of his people is part of that perfection.

Think of the people you know who are married. There is an appropriate measure of jealousy that a husband and wife should have for each other because they love each other and want to keep their marriage as an exclusive relationship. God feels the same way in regard to his relationship with his people—he is right to jealously guard the relationship he has with the people who belong to him.

The fact that God is jealous shows us how passionate he is about us. He loves us and wants us to love him in return.

DISCUSSION STARTERS

- Have you ever felt jealous about the attention someone gave to another person? What was that like?
- What are some differences between our jealousy and God's jealousy? (Think of both the reasons for the jealousy and the way it is expressed.)
- What things in your life might make God jealous for your affection?

THE DEVIL'S FOOTHOLD

You must all be quick to listen, slow to speak, and slow to get angry. Human anger does not produce the righteousness God desires.

JAMES 1:19-20

"Don't sin by letting anger control you." Don't let the sun go down while you are still angry, for anger gives a foothold to the devil.

EPHESIANS 4:26-27

People with understanding control their anger; a hot temper shows great foolishness.

PROVERBS 14:29

Do you ever find yourself "practicing" things you'd like to say to someone you're angry with? We want to be ready to win the war of words! We also talk to other people about what and who has made us angry, wanting them to take our side and feel outraged on our behalf. All the while, we keep throwing logs on the fire of our anger, building our case and assuming the worst about the other person's motives and actions.

Anger is a natural reaction when we feel threatened or injured. But then we have a choice about what we are going to do with that feeling. Will we replay our hurts over and over in our heads, plotting and imagining how good it would feel to put those people in their place? Or will we refuse to allow the poison of anger to rot us on the inside?

We do not have to let anger control us when someone does something that hurts or angers us. We will be tempted to be consumed by this feeling, but we can refuse to give in to that temptation. While anger may be a natural reaction in many situations—and may even be justified by our circumstances—Jesus is all about transforming us on the inside so that we are no longer bound to do what comes naturally. The Holy Spirit in us empowers us to respond supernaturally. He gives us the strength we need to stop demanding what we think we deserve from other people and start receiving his grace and mercy so we can extend it to others.

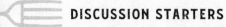

DISCUSSION STARTERS

- What are some ways our anger comes out?
- When someone is angry with you, what do you want him or her to do?
- What do we need to do or tell ourselves in order to let go of anger?

ARE ALL RELIGIONS THE SAME?

There is salvation in no one else! God has given
no other name under heaven by which we must
be saved.

ACTS 4:12

Jesus told him, "I am the way, the truth, and the life.
No one can come to the Father except through me."

JOHN 14:6

There is only one God and one Mediator who can
reconcile God and humanity—the man Christ Jesus.
He gave his life to purchase freedom for everyone.
This is the message God gave to the world at just the
right time.

1 TIMOTHY 2:5-6

L et's say your grandmother lives on the other side of the country, and you're going to take a trip in the car to see her. Imagine that you asked someone for directions, and that person told you that you could take any road you wanted to take and it would get you to her house. Would that make sense?

Many people in the world believe that all those who follow any religion with sincerity will eventually end up at the same place. They think that all religions are equally true, have the same basic goals, and get a person to the same destination—heaven. They claim that it's arrogant to try to convert people from one religion to another and that our common goal should be to make the world a better place by practicing our own various religions and viewing all other religions as equally true or valid.

But does it make sense that Buddhism, Hinduism, Islam, Judaism, and Christianity all represent valid paths to the same destination or that all these religions could be equally true? Of course not. All religions are not the same, and all religions do not point to the One True God. At the heart of every religion is a particular way of defining who God is and why we're here. At the center of Christianity is the person and work of Jesus Christ. The One True God has declared that the one way to know him is through his Son, Jesus. This is the only path that will lead us to God.

DISCUSSION STARTERS

- What are some beliefs you've heard from people of other religions that are different from what the Bible teaches?
- Why is the suggestion that all paths lead to God appealing? Why is it impossible?
- How can we stand firm in our belief that Jesus is the only way to know God, without arguing or coming across as rude?

BUT I'M A GOOD PERSON!

The LORD observed the extent of human wickedness on the earth, and he saw that everything they thought or imagined was consistently and totally evil.

GENESIS 6:5

The human heart is the most deceitful of all things, and desperately wicked. Who really knows how bad it is?

JEREMIAH 17:9

The LORD looks down from heaven on the entire human race; he looks to see if anyone is truly wise, if anyone seeks God. But no, all have turned away; all have become corrupt. No one does good, not a single one!

PSALM 14:2-3

Have you ever seen a TV interview of the friends and family members of someone who has committed a terrible crime? They often say to the interviewer, "I don't know how this happened! He's really a good person!" They see the greed that drove the person to steal or the hate that pushed him or her to harm someone as a surprising exception to the person's basic character and natural tendencies.

But is that really true? Are we basically good people who occasionally do bad things? Or are we thoroughly bad people who occasionally do good things?

The Bible is like a mirror that we look into, and it shows us how we really are. And while we want to think that we are basically good, so that we can save face and feel good about ourselves, the Bible says that we are "totally evil," "desperately wicked," and "corrupt."

But the Bible also has very good news for bad people. If you're a bad person—if even the best things you've done have been tainted by your own sinful motives and thoughts, then you are the kind of person Jesus saves. Only bad people have any need to be saved. If you, instead, see yourself as a basically good person who may have made a mistake or two—if you are a person who deep down believes that God is lucky to have someone like you on his team—you are saying that you really don't need a Savior. To believe you are a good person is to think you have no need for God. But to acknowledge that you are not good enough, on your own, to be accepted into God's presence, is the first step toward becoming someone who can enjoy receiving the goodness of Jesus.

DISCUSSION STARTERS

- What does it mean to be a "good person"?
- How good does a person have to be to be accepted by God?
- Why do you think it is hard for us to accept that we are not really good?

_____

_____

_____

_____

_____

_____

_____

_____

_____

_____

ABANDONED

At about three o'clock, Jesus called out with a loud voice, "*Eli, Eli, lema sabachthani?*" which means "My God, my God, why have you abandoned me?"

MATTHEW 27:46

My God, my God, why have you abandoned me? Why are you so far away when I groan for help?

PSALM 22:1

No, I will not abandon you as orphans—I will come to you.

JOHN 14:18

Have you ever seen a story on the news about a baby who has been left on the doorstep of a church or a hospital or a police station? For whatever reason, the baby's mother couldn't take care of the baby and abandoned him or her.

It's hard to think about parents abandoning children they were meant to love. Now imagine God the Father abandoning his own Son. That's even more difficult to understand, isn't it? It sounds impossible, because we know how much God loves his Son. And yet there was a painful point in time when God turned his back on Jesus. *Why would he do that?* we wonder. And Jesus wondered too, crying out from the cross, "My God, why have you abandoned me?"

But God had to abandon Jesus. When all our sin—all the jealousy, anger, and rebellion, all the lying, stealing, and having bad attitudes, all the times we say things we know we shouldn't—was all laid on Jesus, God could not look on that sin. He had to turn away.

But Jesus was not ultimately abandoned by his Father. Jesus spoke to his Father again from the cross, shouting, "Father, I entrust my spirit into your hands!" (Luke 23:46). Though Jesus was abandoned on the Cross because of our sin, he was not abandoned forever. Once the price for sin was paid, he was welcomed into God's presence. And because Jesus was abandoned, it means we never will be. We, too, will one day be welcomed into the presence of God.

DISCUSSION STARTERS

- Have you ever felt abandoned or alone? Were you truly abandoned?
- What does God's abandonment of Jesus on the cross tell us about how God feels about sin?
- How do we know that God will never abandon us because of our sin?

BELIEVING WITHOUT SEEING

Jesus told him, "You believe because you have seen me. Blessed are those who believe without seeing me."

JOHN 20:29

You love him even though you have never seen him. Though you do not see him now, you trust him; and you rejoice with a glorious, inexpressible joy. The reward for trusting him will be the salvation of your souls.

1 PETER 1:8-9

Faith is the confidence that what we hope for will actually happen; it gives us assurance about things we cannot see.

HEBREWS 11:1

Some people say they'll only believe something if they can prove it or if they can see it with their own eyes. If they can't see it, touch it, hear it, or prove it some other way, they won't believe.

Did you know that Jesus is understanding when it comes to people who have a hard time believing in what they can't see? He showed us that when he was willing to give proof to his disciple Thomas. Thomas said he wouldn't believe that Jesus had risen from the dead unless he touched Jesus' hands where the nails had been and Jesus' side where the spear had wounded him. When Jesus appeared to Thomas, he said, "Put your finger here, and look at my hands. Put your hand into the wound in my side. Don't be faithless any longer. Believe!" And Thomas said, "My Lord and my God!" (John 20:27-28).

Then Jesus responded that those who believe without seeing him are blessed. Jesus knew a time was coming when all who believed in him would do so without the benefit of seeing him with their eyes or touching him with their hands. This is why he gives us the gift of faith. Faith gives us the confidence to believe in a Jesus we have never seen with our physical eyes.

DISCUSSION STARTERS

- Can you think of anything you believe in that you've never seen with your eyes? How about love? the law of gravity? What else?
- What do you think Jesus meant when he said that those who believe without seeing are blessed?
- How would you have expected Jesus to respond to Thomas's request for proof? How does it make you feel to know that Jesus responded this way?

TEMPTED LIKE WE ARE

Jesus was led by the Spirit into the wilderness to be tempted there by the devil.

MATTHEW 4:1

Because he himself suffered when he was tempted, he is able to help those who are being tempted.

HEBREWS 2:18, NIV

We do not have a high priest who is unable to sympathize with our weaknesses, but we have one who has been tempted in every way, just as we are—yet was without sin.

HEBREWS 4:15, NIV

We're naturally skeptical of anyone who offers advice or opinions if they've never experienced what we're experiencing. What athlete wants coaching tips from someone who has never played the game? Who wants to trust a nurse who says, "It won't hurt a bit," if she has never had a shot?

This is why it is helpful to know that Jesus, the one who calls us to flee from sin, knows what it is like to be tempted by sin. Jesus understands how hard it can be to say "no" to what may seem harmless but will ultimately bring ruin.

We tend to think that Jesus had some sort of advantage on us when it comes to temptation because he was fully God as well as being fully human. But Jesus faced temptation as a human being. When he was led into the wilderness to be tempted by the devil, he faced temptation, not with any advantage, but at great disadvantage. He was physically weakened by hunger, yet he refused to misuse the power God had given to him to feed himself. He refused to take hold of the glory God had promised to him without experiencing the Cross that was ahead for him.

There in the wilderness Jesus showed us how to resist temptation—by drawing on God's Word to demonstrate Satan's false promise in it. And since we know he did this as a human being, we know that we can face and reject temptation too. Because Jesus knows what it is like to experience the pressure of temptation, he doesn't take lightly our struggles with sin. Jesus was tempted in all the ways we are, and therefore he deals gently with us.

DISCUSSION STARTERS

- Who do you usually take advice from? Why do you trust these people?
- Is it possible to resist temptation? How?
- Read Matthew 4:1-11. How does Jesus fight temptation in these verses? How can we use the same weapons to fight temptation?

FINDING YOUR WAY OUT

The temptations in your life are no different from what others experience. And God is faithful. He will not allow the temptation to be more than you can stand. When you are tempted, he will show you a way out so that you can endure.

1 CORINTHIANS 10:13

Keep watch and pray, so that you will not give in to temptation. For the spirit is willing, but the body is weak.

MARK 14:38

Those who live only to satisfy their own sinful nature will harvest decay and death from that sinful nature. But those who live to please the Spirit will harvest everlasting life from the Spirit.

GALATIANS 6:8

Before an airplane takes off, a flight attendant shows passengers how to buckle their seat belts and put on an oxygen mask. He or she usually points out lights that will come on along the floor of the aircraft in the event of a power failure or fire, pointing passengers to the nearest exit. It's good to have an exit strategy in place before things get hot! It's also wise to have an exit strategy for when the temptation to sin heats up in your life. We all need a practical plan for getting away from what will hurt us—and perhaps even destroy us.

The first strategy is to avoid what tempts us in the first place, if at all possible. "Hold on to what is good. Stay away from every kind of evil" (1 Thessalonians 5:21-22). Most of us know our own weaknesses, so we know what situations to avoid that bring us tremendous temptation. Second, we should quickly say a firm no to thoughts of temptation rather than tossing the idea around in our minds, fanning its flame. "Resist the devil, and he will flee from you" (James 4:7). We should talk back to the temptation with what we know is true, with what God has promised us. We can focus our thoughts on the promises and joys of Christ until the temptation is exposed for the lie it is and until we want to please God more than we want to sin. Then we must get busy doing something productive and good, replacing our passion for something sinful with a passion for doing something pleasing to God.

DISCUSSION STARTERS

- What's the closest you've ever been to a fire? Do you have a plan for getting out of your house in case of fire?
- Give some examples of what it means to "talk back" to temptation.
- Based on your experiences, how is pleasing God more satisfying than giving in to sin?

WHO ARE MY ENEMIES?

You are my strength; I wait for you to rescue me, for you, O God, are my fortress. In his unfailing love, my God will stand with me. He will let me look down in triumph on all my enemies.

PSALM 59:9-10

If you want to be a friend of the world, you make yourself an enemy of God.

JAMES 4:4

The last enemy to be destroyed is death.

1 CORINTHIANS 15:26

When we think about enemies, we might think of classmates or coworkers who seem out to get us, competitors who want to ruin us, rivals who want to defeat us, or people who have hurt us. We might think of those who disagree with our ideas and oppose our agendas.

The Bible talks about enemies a lot—especially in Old Testament stories about Israel's battles. When we read the Psalms, it can be confusing to figure out who the enemies are that the psalmists ask God to protect them from. Some of the things the biblical writers ask God to do to their enemies we wouldn't wish on anyone!

It helps to understand that the children of Israel and their God-appointed leaders were God's chosen people. Friends of the children of Israel were friends of God. Enemies of Israel were enemies of God.

God wants to give his people victory over their enemies. But our true enemies are not usually people. Unbelief is an enemy. Our worldly desires are enemies. Our ultimate enemy is sin, which has the power to keep us in slavery and to destroy us for good. But God empowers us to overcome all these enemies—anything that would turn us away from him. He gives his people victory over these things by joining us to Jesus Christ who has defeated sin and death.

DISCUSSION STARTERS

- Are there certain people you think of as enemies at times? Are there some people you once thought of as enemies who are now your friends?
- According to Romans 5:6-11, who are God's enemies? What has God done for them?
- Are there any spiritual enemies you need to keep up your guard against?

_____

_____

_____

_____

_____

_____

_____

_____

_____

_____

_____

_____

_____

_____

FAMOUS FOR OBEDIENCE

Everyone knows that you are obedient to the Lord.
This makes me very happy. I want you to be wise
in doing right and to stay innocent of any wrong.

ROMANS 16:19

I thank my God through Jesus Christ for all of you,
because your faith in him is being talked about all
over the world.

ROMANS 1:8

Do everything without complaining and arguing, so
that no one can criticize you. Live clean, innocent
lives as children of God, shining like bright lights in
a world full of crooked and perverse people.

PHILIPPIANS 2:14-15

Turn on the TV or go online or look at the headlines on magazines, and what do you see? Stories and photographs of celebrities. We're a society obsessed with famous people. We love to read about their secrets, their daily habits, and their conflicts with other people. Things that should bring them shame actually get them bigger headlines and more attention.

The Bible tells us that there is something we should be known for—something that might not make headlines but should identify those of us who call ourselves Christians. Our faithful obedience. We should be famous for living pure lives that stand out from the way people around us live without any thought of God.

Jesus said, "Let your good deeds shine out for all to see, so that everyone will praise your heavenly Father (Matthew 5:16). When we deny ourselves or forgive others because of our love for Jesus, people notice. And when they do, it's God who gets the glory. As we live day to day in dramatic contrast to the way everyone around us lives—as we break free from the power of sin—people pay attention. The genuineness of our faith gets talked about, and God gets the praise he deserves.

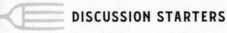

DISCUSSION STARTERS

- What kinds of things do people do that make them famous?
- Who do you know who is "famous" for being obedient to God?
- In the long run, what are the results of worldly fame? What are the results of obedient living?

_____

_____

_____

_____

_____

_____

_____

_____

_____

_____

_____

_____

GOD AS HE IS

The LORD passed in front of Moses, calling out,
"Yahweh! The LORD! The God of compassion and
mercy! I am slow to anger and filled with unfailing
love and faithfulness."

EXODUS 34:6

I will pour out my fury on them, consuming them
with the fire of my anger. I will heap on their heads
the full penalty for all their sins. I, the Sovereign
LORD, have spoken!

EZEKIEL 22:31

He was merciful and forgave their sins and did not
destroy them all. Many times he held back his anger
and did not unleash his fury!

PSALM 78:38

There are some ice cream parlors where you can make your own mix of flavors. You ask the person behind the counter to add a lot of fudge, a few nuts, perhaps a dash of cinnamon—and you have your own unique flavor of ice cream.

Some people think God's character is like that ice cream—a mixture of various qualities in various amounts, with more of some ingredients than others. Some think of him as mostly love with a little justice thrown in. Others might think of him as mostly a giver who also makes a few demands. But God is not a bunch of traits mixed together in varying amounts. While it's true that some actions of God show certain characteristics more obviously, God's whole being includes every one of his attributes. He is love. He is mercy. He is justice. He is truth. He is beauty. He is completely all of those things, and much more. Every attribute of God that we can find in the Bible is true of all of God, all the time. No single attribute is more important or more influential than all the others. His love is not more important than his justice. His righteousness does not take precedence over his patience.

We have a hard time seeing God as he truly is in his completeness. Paul says, "All that I know now is partial and incomplete, but then I will know everything completely, just as God now knows me completely" (1 Corinthians 13:12). Someday we'll see and know God in the fullness of all that he is. And we will not be able to keep from worshipping him with all that we are.

DISCUSSION STARTERS

- How would you answer if someone asked you what God is like?
- Which attributes of God do we usually emphasize?
- Which attributes do we tend to ignore or pay less attention to?

YOUR
NEW NAME

Your name will no longer be Jacob. From now on you will be called Israel, because you have fought with God and with men and have won.

GENESIS 32:28

The nations will see your righteousness. World leaders will be blinded by your glory. And you will be given a new name by the LORD's own mouth.

ISAIAH 62:2

I will give to each one a white stone, and on the stone will be engraved a new name that no one understands except the one who receives it.

REVELATION 2:17

Have you ever met someone who has changed his or her name? Many women change their name when they get married to take their husbands' last name. Some people change their name because they don't like their birth name or because they want to officially go by some other name instead.

One of the early followers of God was named Abram, which means "father of many." Now if you think about it, Abram had a name that just didn't fit. He had only one son, and his wife was way past the age of having children. People probably laughed at the irony of his name. But then God changed his name to one that seemed even more ridiculous: Abraham, which means "father of many nations."

In Hebrew there is a single shortened character that represents the name of God. When God changed Abram to Abraham, he simply added the character for his own name into Abram's name. He did the same thing with Abram's wife when he changed her name from Sarai to Sarah. When God gave them new names, he literally placed his own name in theirs.

This is an outward sign of what God does on the inside of people. He changed Jacob's name to Israel, and he changed Simon's name to Peter. God puts his personal stamp on us and his Spirit in us so we are not the same people we once were apart from his power. When you are truly in Christ, he puts himself *in* you.

DISCUSSION STARTERS

- If you were going to change your name, what would you change it to? Why?
- How was God's power evident in the lives of other people whose names were changed by God? (Think of Jacob and Simon.)
- Revelation 2:17 says that God is going to give all of us new names in heaven. What do you think that might mean?

HOW DO YOU LOVE GOD?

You must love the LORD your God with all your heart, all your soul, all your mind, and all your strength.

MARK 12:30

Jesus told them, "If God were your Father, you would love me."

JOHN 8:42

Those who obey God's word truly show how completely they love him. That is how we know we are living in him.

1 JOHN 2:5

Have you ever met a couple in love? They can't get through a conversation without talking about the other person. They see everything about their lives in relationship to that person. They not only talk fondly about the one they love, but they also look forward to talking to him or her—not out of any sense of duty, but because they want to share the ups and downs of their days, their deepest thoughts and feelings. They look to the future and smile with a sense of satisfaction and anticipation about life together. They can't stand it when something comes between them, and they'll do whatever is necessary to make things right again.

This kind of love helps us understand what the greatest commandment in the Bible means—love the Lord your God with all your heart, soul, mind, and strength. In other words, we are to love God with every part of our beings—our emotions, our thoughts, our speech, and our actions. God knows what our souls need most and what will satisfy our souls most—to love God freely and deeply.

What does it mean to love God? Loving God includes obeying all his commands, believing everything in his Word, thanking him for all his gifts, enjoying all that he is. We respond to his great love for us by embracing his covenant promises from the heart.

DISCUSSION STARTERS

- What does it mean to say you love another person?
- How is loving God similar to loving another person? How is it different?
- How can you learn to love God more? What are some specific ways you can show that love?

CELEBRATE DEPENDENCE DAY

We think you ought to know, dear brothers and sisters, about the trouble we went through in the province of Asia. We were crushed and overwhelmed beyond our ability to endure, and we thought we would never live through it. In fact, we expected to die. But as a result, we stopped relying on ourselves and learned to rely only on God, who raises the dead.

2 CORINTHIANS 1:8-9

This is what the LORD says: "Cursed are those who put their trust in mere humans, who rely on human strength and turn their hearts away from the LORD."

JEREMIAH 17:5

The LORD is good to those who depend on him, to those who search for him.

LAMENTATIONS 3:25

"**I** can do it myself! I don't need any help!" This is the voice of independence. It is inside each one of us, and it has run in our families as far back as Adam and Eve, who wanted to be like God rather than being dependent on God for everything. They had their own ideas about what they needed for a good life, and their desires for independence live on in us.

But according to Jesus, our natural desires for independence don't serve us well in developing a relationship with God. In Matthew 18:3, Jesus says, "I tell you the truth, unless you turn from your sins and become like little children, you will never get into the Kingdom of Heaven." What does it mean to become like little children? It means that we are dependent on God as our heavenly Father, rather than stubbornly and independently thinking we can take care of ourselves. The independent person says, "I'm in charge of my life. I'm free to do what I please and choose what I want. I will take care of myself. I really don't need God's provision or protection. And I really don't need Christ's righteousness. Mine is good enough."

The world tells us to give ourselves a pep talk, saying, *I can do it. I just need to believe in myself.* But Jesus says, "Apart from me you can do nothing" (John 15:5). Rather than seeking to become more self-confident, we need to strive to become more God-reliant. Rather than seeking and celebrating independence, it is actually a willingness to be dependent on God that is worth celebrating.

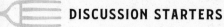

DISCUSSION STARTERS

- What are some things you can't do for yourself?
- How can prayer encourage our sense of dependence on God?
- What types of experiences help to deepen our dependence on God?

GROWING UP

Christ will make his home in your hearts as you trust in him. Your roots will grow down into God's love and keep you strong.

EPHESIANS 3:17

Since Christ suffered physical pain, you must arm yourselves with the same attitude he had, and be ready to suffer, too. For if you have suffered physically for Christ, you have finished with sin. You won't spend the rest of your lives chasing your own desires, but you will be anxious to do the will of God.

1 PETER 4:1-2

You know that when your faith is tested, your endurance has a chance to grow. So let it grow, for when your endurance is fully developed, you will be perfect and complete, needing nothing.

JAMES 1:3-4

Nobody wants to suffer. In fact, most of us would have to admit that we spend a lot of energy doing everything we can to avoid pain. But suffering should not surprise us. Scripture tells us over and over to expect it.

We might think that the best method to grow up spiritually is to attend Bible studies and learn everything we can about the Bible. But God's method of choice to make us spiritually mature seems to be suffering. However, suffering itself doesn't do the job. It is how we respond to the suffering that determines if the pain will become fertile ground for real growth. Growth comes when we respond to the major heartaches and minor difficulties in our lives with an attitude of endurance. Growth comes when we can say in the face of suffering, "This will not diminish my faith or trust in God. It will only cause me to dig deeper in my faith and trust him more fully."

So when life is hard, the most important question we must ask is, how will we look at our pain? Will we see it as God falling down on the job of keeping our lives pain free? Or will we see it for what it is—a tool God is using to strengthen our faith?

DISCUSSION STARTERS

- When parents discipline their children, what is their goal?
- Why do you think people tend to see their suffering as a sign that God doesn't care instead of as a sign that God loves them?
- Do you know anyone who is stronger in his or her faith in God because of an experience of suffering?

HOW DO YOU HANDLE CRITICISM?

Humble yourselves under the mighty power of God, and at the right time he will lift you up in honor.

1 PETER 5:6

When Peter came to Antioch, I had to oppose him to his face, for what he did was very wrong.

GALATIANS 2:11

Whoever learns from correction is wise. . . . If you listen to constructive criticism, you will be at home among the wise.

PROVERB 15:5, 31

What do you do when someone criticizes or corrects you? Do you go with your first instinct to defend your actions or opinions? Do you criticize the other person in return? Do you point out the flaw in the other person's argument or the way it was presented? Or do you listen to it, evaluate it, and learn from it?

Nobody likes to be criticized or corrected. There's a sting to it. But if we quickly dismiss a correction or argue with it, we miss out on an opportunity to learn from what our critics have had the courage to say to us.

As sinful humans, we have an amazing ability to convince ourselves of our own rightness and to justify what we know isn't right. We can be blind to our own sin, oblivious to our real motives, and unaware of how we might be hurting others. But others can often see what we don't. So we have to be willing to humbly listen to what they have to say. Sometimes the truth hurts, and it's easier to blame the person who points out our problem than to face the reality of our own sins and weaknesses.

But criticism delivered in a loving manner is really a gift to us if we are willing to receive it. In fact, even criticism delivered with the wrong motives in the worst of ways can be a gift too, depending on how we respond to it. So when we're criticized, we should consider it carefully, looking for the truth about ourselves that needs to be faced and rejecting the untruth that needs to be dismissed. We can learn from it, and then we can let it go.

DISCUSSION STARTERS

- What does it feel like when someone criticizes you?
- How can a person receive and respond to criticism with humility?
- How can someone's criticism be a gift from God?

WHAT DOES GOODNESS LOOK LIKE?

Moses responded, "Then show me your glorious presence."

The LORD replied, "I will make all my goodness pass before you, and I will call out my name, Yahweh, before you."

EXODUS 33:18-19

Surely your goodness and unfailing love will pursue me all the days of my life.

PSALM 23:6

How great is the goodness you have stored up for those who fear you.

You lavish it on those who come to you for protection, blessing them before the watching world.

PSALM 31:19

"That's good!" we say, talking about a meal we've eaten, a new movie we've seen, or a plan someone has suggested. We see ourselves as judges who determine what is good and what is not. We label things as good or bad based on a standard inside ourselves, one that is sometimes shaped mostly by our personal preferences or the culture around us.

But God has shown us exactly what goodness is. God himself is the standard and the definition of goodness. When Moses asked to see God, God gave him only a glimpse of himself. He told Moses he would make all of his goodness pass before him. Goodness is the essence of who God is. He is the very definition of goodness.

Sometimes our circumstances seem like anything but evidence of God's goodness. But that's because we tend to define God by what *we* have deemed good. We have to turn that around. We have to learn to define goodness by who God is and what he does. God is completely, abundantly, perfectly, and forever good. God himself is the standard by which we should compare anything we want to label as good.

DISCUSSION STARTERS

- What are some things God says are good? What are some things he says are bad?
- What sometimes causes us to question God's goodness?
- What difference does it make if God himself becomes our standard for what is good?

KIND AND SEVERE

I am slow to anger and filled with unfailing love and faithfulness. I lavish unfailing love to a thousand generations. I forgive iniquity, rebellion, and sin. But I do not excuse the guilty. I lay the sins of the parents upon their children and grandchildren; the entire family is affected—even children in the third and fourth generations.

EXODUS 34:6-7

Don't you see how wonderfully kind, tolerant, and patient God is with you? . . . Can't you see that his kindness is intended to turn you from your sin? But because you are stubborn and refuse to turn from your sin, you are storing up terrible punishment for yourself.

ROMANS 2:4-5

God is both kind and severe. He is severe toward those who disobeyed, but kind to you if you continue to trust in his kindness.

ROMANS 11:22

Did you ever play the game Red Rover? "Red Rover, Red Rover, send Mary right over!" one side says in unison. And then Mary comes running in response.

When the Bible tells us that God is both kind and severe, we can think of it a bit like the two opposite sides of the Red Rover game. Because we have sinned, we find ourselves on the side of God's severity. We find ourselves vulnerable to his judgment. But in the gospel, the kindness of God calls out to each one of us, saying, "Come over! Come to me and experience my kindness toward you even though you've done wrong." And who wouldn't want to run away from the severity of God—a place of certain judgment—into the arms of abundant forgiveness, generosity, freedom, and joy?

Because God is completely holy and perfectly just, he must be appropriately severe in judging sin. But God is also generously kind. That's why he gives us time. He's patient. He calls out to us to run away from his holy judgment and toward his kindness. All who refuse to run to him can expect to experience his judgment. But all who run to him can expect to experience his kindness for all eternity.

DISCUSSION STARTERS

- How do you see both God's kindness and severity in these verses?
- Why do you suppose we only like to think about God's kindness?
- Why is it good for people—even believers—to think about God's severity?

HONORING GOD WITH YOUR BODY

Do not let any part of your body become an instrument of evil to serve sin. Instead, give yourselves completely to God, for you were dead, but now you have new life. So use your whole body as an instrument to do what is right for the glory of God.

ROMANS 6:13

Give your bodies to God because of all he has done for you. Let them be a living and holy sacrifice—the kind he will find acceptable.

ROMANS 12:1

Don't you realize that your body is the temple of the Holy Spirit, who lives in you and was given to you by God? You do not belong to yourself, for God bought you with a high price. So you must honor God with your body.

1 CORINTHIANS 6:19-20

Isn't it amazing how billions of people on this earth are made up of all the same body parts, and yet we all look so different? Some people's bodies are strong and firm; some are weak and feeble. Some are large; some are small. Some are young and some are old. And amazingly, no matter the size or shape or age of our bodies, we can all use our bodies to honor God.

How do we honor God with our bodies?

All of us are stewards, or managers, of the bodies God has given us. We're to use every resource at our disposal—including our bodies—to bring honor to God. Giving your body to God for his use means that you give him your eyes, your tongue, your hands, and your feet rather than giving your eyes, your tongue, your hands, and your feet to sin. It means that you give to God the best of your body's energy, the best of your mind's intellect, and the best of your heart's passions. Everything you do with your body shows that Christ is more precious to you than anything else. Don't think that you can give your heart to God and not give every part of your body to him too. Either you belong to God—heart, soul, and body—or you don't really belong to him at all.

DISCUSSION STARTERS

- Think through the various parts of your body. What can you do with those parts of your body to honor God? What actions would dishonor him?
- Do you think a focus on wise eating habits and good health is honoring to God? At what point does it become dishonoring to him?
- Why do you think God wants our bodies, too, and not just our hearts?

TRUE BEAUTY

There was nothing beautiful or majestic about his appearance, nothing to attract us to him.

ISAIAH 53:2

You should clothe yourselves instead with the beauty that comes from within, the unfading beauty of a gentle and quiet spirit, which is so precious to God.

1 PETER 3:4

One thing I ask of the LORD, this is what I seek: that I may dwell in the house of the LORD all the days of my life, to gaze upon the beauty of the LORD and to seek him in his temple.

PSALM 27:4, NIV

There is a saying that has been around since the third century BC: "Beauty is in the eye of the beholder." If this is true, then there is no objective source for deciding if something is beautiful or ugly—it is all a matter of personal preference or opinion. But is that true?

Built into each one of us is a longing for beauty. We get pleasure from seeing beauty in a green valley, a marble statue, or the perfect basketball dunk. We experience the beauty of a piece of music, words well spoken, or the taste of a ripe, red strawberry. Seeing and experiencing beauty all around us adds joy to life. But all these things we find to be beautiful are really just reflections or pointers to a greater beauty.

God himself is ultimate beauty. He's the definition of beauty, the standard of beauty that we judge everything against. And our longing for beauty is really a longing for God himself.

A great painting is beautiful not because of the isolated colors or shapes or textures but because of the way all those elements interact with each other. It is the same with the person of God. What makes God beautiful is not just his attributes; it's their relationship to each other—their perfect harmony and balance and completeness. All his perfections are on display in creation and in the Bible, and when we are able to catch a glimpse of how his perfections relate to one another, it takes our breath away.

DISCUSSION STARTERS

- What or who is beautiful to you?
- How does what we see as beautiful affect what we become?
- Why do you think it seems a little strange to say that God is beautiful?

STICKING TOGETHER

You must not commit adultery.

DEUTERONOMY 5:18

Give honor to marriage, and remain faithful to one another in marriage. God will surely judge people who are immoral and those who commit adultery.

HEBREWS 13:4

You have heard the commandment that says, "You must not commit adultery." But I say, anyone who even looks at a woman with lust has already committed adultery with her in his heart.

MATTHEW 5:27-28

Have you ever sealed an envelope and then tried to open it again? As you try to pry it open, it rips and tears, with some parts of the flap still sticking to the envelope. This is similar to what happens when a person has sex outside of marriage. While our culture today suggests that sex can be casual and non-committal, sexual intercourse attaches people to each other in a profound way. Television and movies don't portray the pain involved in becoming sexually involved with someone you are not married to and then separating from each other.

God wants to save us from this pain. His design is for us to become "attached" to one person we can be completely committed to for life. Jesus said, "'A man leaves his father and mother and is joined to his wife, and the two are united into one.' Since they are no longer two but one, let no one split apart what God has joined together" (Matthew 19:5-6). God knows that a marriage with two people seeking to be faithful to him and to each other is what will honor him and make us deeply happy. He also knows that attaching ourselves to people outside of marriage will ultimately bring us only pain and regret.

God intends for marriage to be a living illustration of the kind of faithful love relationship Christ has with his bride—the church. He wants the world to be able to see the faithful, exclusive way Jesus loves his people reflected in how we love each other.

DISCUSSION STARTERS

- How does it hurt a relationship when one person breaks his or her promises?
- In addition to sexual faithfulness, what does it mean to be faithful in marriage?
- How does adultery show selfishness as well as a lack of trust in God?

TIME FOR WORK

You have six days each week for your ordinary work.

EXODUS 20:9

Make it your goal to live a quiet life, minding your own business and working with your hands, just as we instructed you before. Then people who are not Christians will respect the way you live, and you will not need to depend on others.

1 THESSALONIANS 4:11-12

We hear that some of you are living idle lives, refusing to work and meddling in other people's business. We command such people and urge them in the name of the Lord Jesus Christ to settle down and work to earn their own living.

2 THESSALONIANS 3:11-12

It is interesting to observe how people respond when they win the lottery. Some of them never go back to work; they see the money they won as their ticket to a life of ease. Others report for work the next day and keep on working. They recognize that meaningful work is about more than a paycheck.

Did you know working is a very godlike thing to do? We read in Genesis that God worked for six days and then rested on the seventh day. When he made Adam, he immediately gave him a job in the Garden—a job he was perfectly suited for, a job that was fulfilling.

We tend to categorize work into spiritual work, like being a missionary or a minister, and secular work, like being a doctor, an engineer, a salesperson, a teacher, or a student. But to God, all work is a calling from him and has dignity. Martin Luther said, "A dairymaid can milk cows to the glory of God." We live in a day and age where certain professions are honored above others. (Have you ever seen "Oscars" given out to police officers or lunchroom cooks or accountants?) But God does not value certain kinds of work more than others like people do. If you do the work God has set before you to do for the glory of God, it has eternal value in God's book.

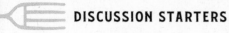

DISCUSSION STARTERS

- What jobs or professions have always fascinated you? How could a person do those jobs to the glory of God?
- Are there some professions that could never bring glory to God?
- Who are some people you know who set a good example of working hard and using their gifts to serve God in their professions?

HE'S GOT THE WHOLE WORLD . . .

All the people of the earth are nothing compared to him. He does as he pleases among the angels of heaven and among the people of the earth.

DANIEL 4:35

The LORD of Heaven's Armies has sworn this oath: "It will all happen as I have planned. It will be as I have decided. . . . I have a plan for the whole earth, a hand of judgment upon all the nations.

ISAIAH 14:24, 26

Because we are united with Christ, we have received an inheritance from God, for he chose us in advance, and he makes everything work out according to his plan.

EPHESIANS 1:11

"**H**e's got the whole world in his hands. He's got the whole world in his hands. . . ." Have you ever sung that song? If God has the whole world in his hands, then he can do whatever he wants with it, right? He's in charge. Jesus affirmed this when he prayed to his Father, "May your will be done on earth, as it is in heaven" (Matthew 6:10).

People talk about God's will a lot, and really there are two aspects about the will of God we need to grasp. Both are true, and both are important to understand and believe in. There is the sovereign will of God—what God has planned for history that always comes to pass, without fail. Then there is the revealed will of God—the way God wants us to live—which is clearly revealed in the Bible. This part of the will of God does not always come to pass because of the fallenness of this world and our disobedience.

The sovereign will of God is the way he works out his divine plan for all things. That includes small things: "Not a single sparrow can fall to the ground without your Father knowing it" (Matthew 10:29). And it includes big things: "The king's heart is like a stream of water directed by the Lord; he guides it wherever he pleases" (Proverbs 21:1). Nothing and no one can hinder God's sovereign will from coming about in the world.

DISCUSSION STARTERS

- Can you think of anything that God does not have in his hands or is not in charge of?
- Can people look back at choices they made or things they did in the past and say that they missed God's will?
- If God is working out his sovereign plan, what is he working all things toward?

FORGIVING THOSE WHO DON'T GET IT

You have heard the law that says, "Love your neighbor" and hate your enemy. But I say, love your enemies! Pray for those who persecute you! In that way, you will be acting as true children of your Father in heaven.

MATTHEW 5:43-45

Jesus said, "Father, forgive them, for they don't know what they are doing."

LUKE 23:34

The wisdom we speak of is the mystery of God— his plan that was previously hidden, even though he made it for our ultimate glory before the world began. But the rulers of this world have not understood it; if they had, they would not have crucified our glorious Lord.

1 CORINTHIANS 2:7-8

When someone does something that hurts you, what is your first reaction? Do you want to hurt that person back? Do you want to make him or her pay, or at least make sure the person understands what he or she has done wrong? Most of us do. It is very hard to forgive someone who just doesn't get what he or she has done that has hurt us or simply is not sorry.

But Jesus proposed a radical way to respond to people who hurt us. He suggested that we pray for them. Jesus himself went beyond preaching this radical forgiveness. He lived it out at the lowest, hardest moment of his life—when he was being nailed to the cross. Hanging on the cross, he asked God the Father to forgive the people who didn't understand what they were doing when they rejected and killed their only source of salvation—the Son of God. Forgiveness is such a difficult thing that we oftentimes think we just can't do it. And the truth is, we don't have enough love on our own to forgive like Jesus did. But he can fill us with his love so that we, too, can forgive those who hurt us—even when they're not sorry and don't even get how they've hurt us. When we are joined to Jesus by faith, the power he had to forgive those who hurt him flows into us so that we have the strength we need to forgive those who hurt us.

DISCUSSION STARTERS

- Does someone have to be sorry in order for you to be willing to forgive him or her?
- When Jesus said, "They don't know what they are doing," what do you think he meant?
- What does Jesus' example tell us about how to respond to those who don't deserve our forgiveness?

YOUR INHERITANCE

You are no longer a slave but God's own child. And since you are his child, God has made you his heir.

GALATIANS 4:7

Since we are his children, we are his heirs. In fact, together with Christ we are heirs of God's glory.

ROMANS 8:17

The Spirit is God's guarantee that he will give us the inheritance he promised and that he has purchased us to be his own people. He did this so we would praise and glorify him.

EPHESIANS 1:14

A "last will and testament" is an important and official legal document that a person writes to let people know what should be done with his or her possessions after that person dies. The people who get that person's belongings or money after he or she dies are called heirs.

God, too, has made up a will and named his heirs. "God promised everything to the Son as an inheritance," says Hebrews 1:2. The heir of all things is Jesus Christ. In the end, Jesus will have all things under his complete control and ownership—all natural resources, all governmental power, all human intelligence, all the riches of the earth. Everything will be under his authority and command.

And while Jesus doesn't have to share his inheritance with anyone, he will! Jesus has promised that he will share all he inherits with everyone who trusts in him. Scripture says that God's children will inherit a home in heaven, an eternal body made for us by God himself, all God's promises, and all the good things of heaven. Someday each one of us will leave this earth and let go of everyone we have loved and everything we have enjoyed. We'll be left with only our eternal inheritance. But we will not be disappointed. The inheritance Jesus will share with us will be everything we've anticipated and more.

DISCUSSION STARTERS

- What kinds of things do people inherit from other people?
- Wills go into effect only after death. On a spiritual level, whose death put our inheritance into effect?
- How can knowing about our inheritance in heaven help us in our battle with materialism? How can it help us endure suffering?

IMPOSSIBLE TO PLEASE?

Faith is the assurance of things hoped for, the conviction of things not seen. For by it the men of old gained approval. By faith we understand that the worlds were prepared by the word of God, so that what is seen was not made out of things which are visible.

HEBREWS 11:1-3, NASB

Without faith it is impossible to please Him, for he who comes to God must believe that He is and that He is a rewarder of those who seek Him.

HEBREWS 11:6, NASB

At last everyone will say, "There truly is a reward for those who live for God; surely there is a God who judges justly here on earth."

PSALM 58:11

Some bosses and teachers are impossible to please. They seem to always find some fault with a person's work or effort. It can be disheartening and discouraging, making that person just want to give up trying.

Some people see God like that—impossible to please. They feel like their efforts to be good enough or do enough for God are never sufficient. But Hebrews 11 tells us clearly how people gain God's approval: by faith. Hebrews describes faith as being sure of God's promises—confident that they are worth looking forward to and living for. Faith is also believing that the one true God who made the world (not just some sort of "higher power") exists. Hebrews 11 says there is something specific we need to believe about this God: "that He is a rewarder of those who seek Him."

God is not a stingy, hard-to-please tyrant or bully. He is a generous rewarder. He gives us the desire to go after him, and then he rewards us for our pursuit of him. What is the reward God gives us? He gives grace and forgiveness. He rewards us with the righteousness of Jesus in place of our failed attempts at being right with God. But the most prized reward he gives us is himself—in closer relationship and clearer understanding.

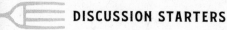

DISCUSSION STARTERS

- What kinds of things do people usually have to do to get a reward?
- Do you see God as difficult to please or as a generous giver? Why?
- What does it mean to seek him, as Hebrews 11:6 tells us to do?

A WORK OF ART

Will the one who contends with the Almighty correct him? Let him who accuses God answer him!

JOB 40:2, NIV

Who are you, a mere human being, to argue with God? Should the thing that was created say to the one who created it, "Why have you made me like this?"

ROMANS 9:20

I . . . found the potter working at his wheel. But the jar he was making did not turn out as he had hoped, so he crushed it into a lump of clay again and started over. Then the LORD gave me this message: "O Israel, can I not do to you as this potter has done to his clay? As the clay is in the potter's hand, so are you in my hand."

JEREMIAH 18:3-6

Have you ever seen an artist in the process of making a piece of art—maybe a drawing or a painting or a quilt? Or have you watched a potter take a lump of wet, messy clay and put it on a potter's wheel? The clay gets spun around while the potter shapes the clay with his or her hands and makes it into a bowl or plate or some other container.

How ridiculous would it be for the clay to tell the potter how it should be shaped and what it should be used for? Or how strange would it be for the canvas to tell the painter what to draw or the fabric to tell the tailor what to sew? That's for the creator to decide!

Throughout Scripture, God uses the picture of a potter making something out of clay to show us how he is shaping us into what he wants us to be.

But sometimes we just don't like how our Creator has made us, do we? We think, *Why did God give me this body? Why didn't he give me that ability? Why isn't he using me that way?* So we have to ask ourselves, *Does God have the right to shape my life according to his own wise purposes, or not?* Though we are tempted to resist, or at least to give him our input and opinion, our answer should be, "Yes! Great Potter, I give you this lump of clay called my life. Use whatever pressure is needed to shape me into something of great worth and beauty in your sight, something ready to display your glory!"

DISCUSSION STARTERS

- What's the most impressive work of art you've seen? What made it so good?
- A potter applies pressure to shape the clay. What pressures has God applied to your life to shape you into someone he can use?
- Is being in God's hands a safe place to be? How do you know?

THE
KINGDOM

One day the Pharisees asked Jesus, "When will the Kingdom of God come?"

Jesus replied, "The Kingdom of God can't be detected by visible signs. You won't be able to say, 'Here it is!' or 'It's over there!' For the Kingdom of God is already among you."

LUKE 17:20-21

Seek the Kingdom of God above all else, and live righteously, and he will give you everything you need.

MATTHEW 6:33

The Kingdom of God is not just a lot of talk; it is living by God's power.

1 CORINTHIANS 4:20

Fairy tales and stories often center on kings and their kingdoms. And what we know from these tales is that in a kingdom, the king is in charge. What he says goes.

Jesus talked a lot about his Kingdom—but the kind of Kingdom he spoke of is different from any other kingdom we've ever heard of. Jesus told people that the Kingdom of God "is already among you," but he also talked about it as something that is coming in the future.

So which is it? Is the Kingdom of God something in the future that we are waiting for, or are we living in it now? The answer is yes. The Kingdom of God has come—but only partly. The Kingdom came in part when Jesus, the King, entered our world and lived out God's purposes for him. But the coming of his Kingdom will be complete only when Jesus returns and destroys evil and its deadly effects on this world for good.

The Kingdom of God is a reality in our lives to the extent that Jesus rules in our hearts. It does not come like a military overthrow that takes power by force. His Kingdom comes to us like a small seed that must be planted so it can blossom. The seed is planted in our lives when we become joined to him by faith, and it grows throughout our lifetime as we submit to his rule in our lives.

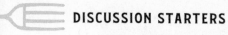

DISCUSSION STARTERS

- What stories can you think of that include kings and kingdoms?
- In what ways is Jesus the same as other kings? In what ways is he different?
- What can we do now to welcome God's Kingdom in the world and in our hearts while we wait for it to be fully completed?

_____

_____

_____

_____

_____

_____

_____

_____

_____

_____

A SPIRITUAL SWEET TOOTH

The laws of the LORD are true; each one is fair. They are more desirable than gold, even the finest gold. They are sweeter than honey, even honey dripping from the comb.

PSALM 19:9-10

When I discovered your words, I devoured them. They are my joy and my heart's delight, for I bear your name, O LORD God of Heaven's Armies.

JEREMIAH 15:16

My child, eat honey, for it is good, and the honeycomb is sweet to the taste. In the same way, wisdom is sweet to your soul. If you find it, you will have a bright future, and your hopes will not be cut short.

PROVERBS 24:13-14

What is the sweetest thing you can think of? Your favorite kind of ice cream? Your favorite candy? Or maybe a rich chocolate cake?

Before there was such a thing as refined sugar, honey was the sweetest taste people ever enjoyed. So when the psalmist was looking for a metaphor that would describe how good the Word of God is, he reached for the best example of sweetness that people in his day were familiar with: honey.

He was saying that the Word of God tastes like the sweetest thing he'd ever tasted.

Reading the Bible and hearing it preached is not meant to be something you don't like but force-feed yourself because you know it's good for you (like brussels sprouts, perhaps!). God intends for his Word to be an invigorating taste sensation, a treat. But sometimes we have to develop a taste for it. We have to take bites of it and chew on it a while, thinking it through, allowing it to work its way through our lives, changing how we think and how we feel.

If the Word of God often seems tasteless or unenjoyable to you, perhaps you might ask God to give you a spiritual sweet tooth. Ask him to give you a taste and an appetite for his Word.

DISCUSSION STARTERS

- What is your favorite sweet food?
- Do you really believe you could get as much pleasure from the Bible as you get from your favorite dessert? How?
- How do you think you will know if God answers your prayer for a spiritual sweet tooth?

THE LORD OF TIME

Remember the things I have done in the past. For I alone am God! I am God, and there is none like me. Only I can tell you the future before it even happens. Everything I plan will come to pass.

ISAIAH 46:9-10

You must not forget this one thing, dear friends: A day is like a thousand years to the Lord, and a thousand years is like a day.

2 PETER 3:8

"I am the Alpha and the Omega—the beginning and the end," says the Lord God. "I am the one who is, who always was, and who is still to come—the Almighty One."

REVELATION 1:8

Have you ever watched a TV show or movie or read a book about people who travel back or forward in time? It is the stuff of science fiction, because we know it is impossible. As humans, we are bound by time. We can't stop it. The clock is always ticking, and the calendar is always moving forward.

But God is not limited by time the way we are—just like he is not bound by gravity or space as we are. He doesn't age like we do. God exists outside of time. And while he sees events in time and acts at particular times in the past and the present and the future, time to him is not a succession of moments or a progression of days. He sees all time as if it just happened.

It's hard to understand, isn't it? Because it is so different from how we experience time, it's hard to wrap our minds around it.

Although God is not bound by time the way we are, the Bible from Genesis to Revelation is a record of the way God has acted over time to redeem his people. Paul writes, "When the right time came, God sent his Son" (Galatians 4:4). He is the Lord who created time. And he is the Lord who rules over time and uses it for his own good and glorious purposes.

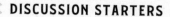

DISCUSSION STARTERS

- If you were like God and could see all events as if they just happened, what past or future event would you most like to see?
- How does understanding God's timelessness increase our confidence in what he says about what is ahead for believers?
- How does this knowledge about God being outside of time help us understand Ephesians 1:4: "Even before he made the world, God loved us and chose us in Christ to be holy"?

GOD IS WITH YOU

I know the LORD is always with me. I will not be shaken, for he is right beside me.

PSALM 16:8

Even when I walk through the darkest valley, I will not be afraid, for you are close beside me. Your rod and your staff protect and comfort me.

PSALM 23:4

Come close to God, and God will come close to you.

JAMES 4:8

Brother Lawrence was a French monk who lived during the 1600s. Because his sense of inner peace was so profound, people were drawn to him. He explained to them that he sought to keep his attention riveted on God, no matter what he was doing, which filled him with peace and joy. He called it the practice of the presence of God. "We should establish ourselves in a sense of God's Presence, by continually conversing with Him. It's a shameful thing to quit His conversation to think of trifles and fooleries," he said. "We need only to recognize God intimately present with us and to address ourselves to Him every moment."*

If we're honest, we have to admit that the promise that God is with us doesn't always seem like such a great deal! Often we don't want God to simply *be* with us. We want him to *do* something for us. The truth is, sometimes we want *what he has to offer* more than we want *him*. We work through our Bible studies to get the answers, and we pray through our lists until our minds wander. Too quickly, we're on to "more important" matters than simply experiencing and enjoying the very real presence of God. He's here, but we've missed him.

God's generous offer of his very presence is his most precious gift to us. The God who made us walks beside us in the highest and lowest points of life. He's there at big events, and he's with us on ordinary afternoons. There is never a time or place when we cannot savor his presence with us.

---

*· For more on Brother Lawrence, see *Practicing the Presence of God* (Orleans, MA: Paraclete Press, 2007).

DISCUSSION STARTERS

- When are some times you'd rather have someone with you than be alone?
- When is it easiest for you to "practice" God's presence? When is it most difficult?
- How could you enjoy and appreciate the presence of God more?

GRATITUDE ON GUARD

The Lord is my strength and shield. I trust him with all my heart. He helps me, and my heart is filled with joy. I burst out in songs of thanksgiving.

PSALM 28:7

Let your roots grow down into him, and let your lives be built on him. Then your faith will grow strong in the truth you were taught, and you will overflow with thankfulness.

COLOSSIANS 2:7

Obscene stories, foolish talk, and coarse jokes—these are not for you. Instead, let there be thankfulness to God.

EPHESIANS 5:4

One of the favorite tourist stops for people visiting London, England, is to watch the changing of the guard at Buckingham Palace. Besides putting on a grand show, the guard actively protects the palace and the queen from anything and anyone who might seek to penetrate the walls of the palace and harm her.

Our hearts and minds are a bit like the queen inside the palace. There are many harmful attitudes that would like to penetrate the walls. Greed. Self-centeredness. Addiction. The feeling that the world owes us. Once inside, these thought patterns wreak havoc on our relationships and steal our joy. If we want to keep them out, we have to place a guard on watch to protect us. But what has the power to protect us from these things?

The guard is gratitude. Ongoing gratitude, expressed in the words we speak and experienced in the way we think— serves as a guard against sinful, harmful attitudes that attack us and try to make themselves at home in us.

It is hard for bitterness to find a foothold in the heart of a grateful person. There's no room for demanding behavior in the life of a grateful person. The same lips that offer thanksgiving are less likely to complain or blame or gossip. Voicing our gratitude humbles us, leaving no room for pride. Expressing gratitude to God builds our faith and confidence in him. Gratitude guards us from the sense of entitlement that would destroy us.

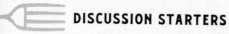

DISCUSSION STARTERS

- What are you especially grateful for?
- When you are grateful for the material things you have, the family you have, and the spiritual blessings you have, how can that help guard against sin?
- How does expressing gratitude out loud help it make its way into our hearts?

CLOTHED
IN HUMILITY

She gave birth to her first child, a son. She wrapped him snugly in strips of cloth and laid him in a manger.

LUKE 2:7

He got up from the table, took off his robe, wrapped a towel around his waist, and poured water into a basin. Then he began to wash the disciples' feet, drying them with the towel he had around him.

JOHN 13:4-5

He took the body down from the cross and wrapped it in a long sheet of linen cloth and laid it in a new tomb that had been carved out of rock.

LUKE 23:53

Most of us like to look good. We like to impress other people, and we realize that what we wear sends a message about ourselves. So we look for clothes that will tell people what we want to say about ourselves.

From the day he was born, Jesus' clothing told us something significant about him. The way he dressed reflected the attitude of his heart: humility. Mary didn't have nice clothes to put on Jesus when he was born. In fact, there were no clothes at all for him—just strips of cloth that were wrapped around him.

When the eternal Son of God became human in the person of Jesus, he chose to take off the robes of glory that were his in heaven. He laid them aside to be wrapped in rags. He "took the humble position of a slave" (Philippians 2:7) instead of seeking to impress. We see this same picture in another scene much later in Jesus' life. The night before he died, Jesus took off his robe and wrapped a towel around his waist. In other words, he dressed like a common slave in his day. Then he began to wash the dusty feet of his disciples. And when he finished he told them, "I have given you an example to follow" (John 13:15).

Jesus shows us what it looks like to clothe ourselves in humility, which is less about what we wear and more about how we serve others.

DISCUSSION STARTERS

- Think about your favorite outfit. What does it say about you?
- Think through Jesus' life and lifestyle. In addition to the way he dressed, what were some other signs that showed his humility?
- What does Philippians 2:3-8 teach us about the humility of Jesus? How we can dress the same way?

ABOUT THE AUTHOR

**Nancy Guthrie** teaches the Bible at her church, Cornerstone Presbyterian Church, in Franklin, Tennessee, at conferences worldwide, and through numerous books and video series. She and her husband, David, are the cohosts of the GriefShare video series used in more than 12,000 churches nationwide and host Respite Retreats for couples who have experienced the death of a child. Guthrie is also the host of Help Me Teach the Bible, a podcast of the Gospel Coalition.

BY NANCY GUTHRIE

BOOKS

Holding On to Hope

The One Year® Book of Hope

Hearing Jesus Speak into Your Sorrow

When Your Family's Lost a Loved One (with David Guthrie)

What Grieving People Wish You Knew about What Really Helps (and What Really Hurts)

One Year® of Dinner Table Devotions and Discussion Starters

The One Year® Book of Discovering Jesus in the Old Testament

Abundant Life in Jesus

The One Year® Praying through the Bible for Your Kids

BOOKS (CONT.)

Seeing Jesus

What Every Child Should Know about Prayer

BIBLE STUDIES

Hoping for Something Better

The Promised One

The Lamb of God

The Son of David

The Wisdom of God

The Word of the Lord

Even Better than Eden

Saints and Scoundrels in the Story of Jesus

CP1149